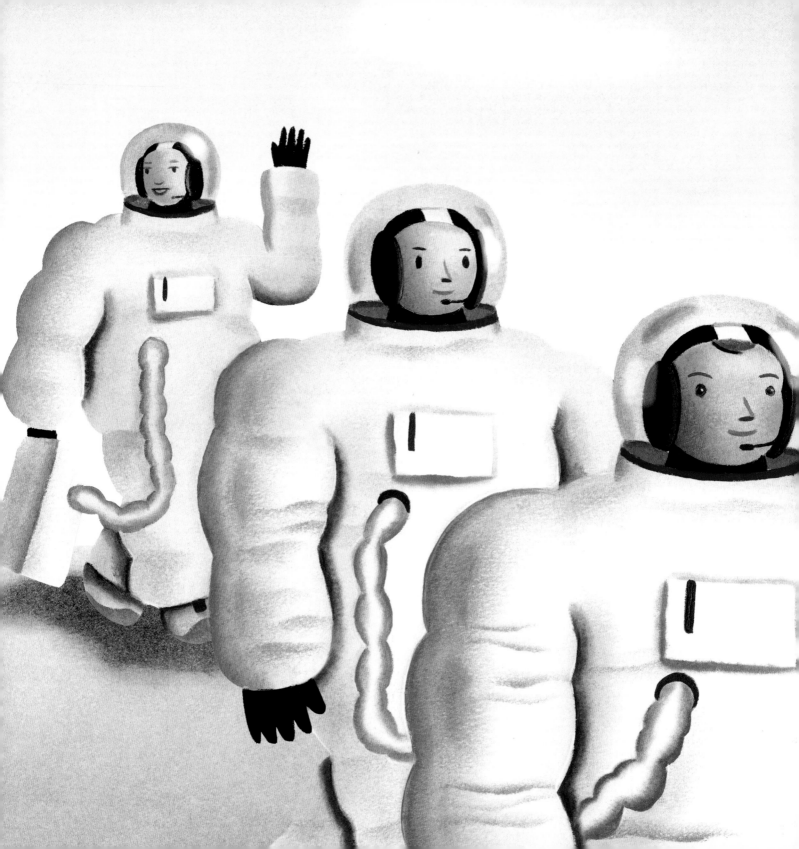

EIGHT DAYS GONE

Linda McReynolds

Illustrated by Ryan O'Rourke

ini Charlesbridge

Hundreds gather.
Hot July.
Spaceship ready—
set to fly.

Launchpad countdown.
Smoke and flame.
Rumbling. Blasting.
Seizing fame.

Rocket orbits.
Engines fire.
Toward the moon.
Soaring higher.

Shrinking planet.
Streaming fast.
Starry darkness.
Sprawling, vast.

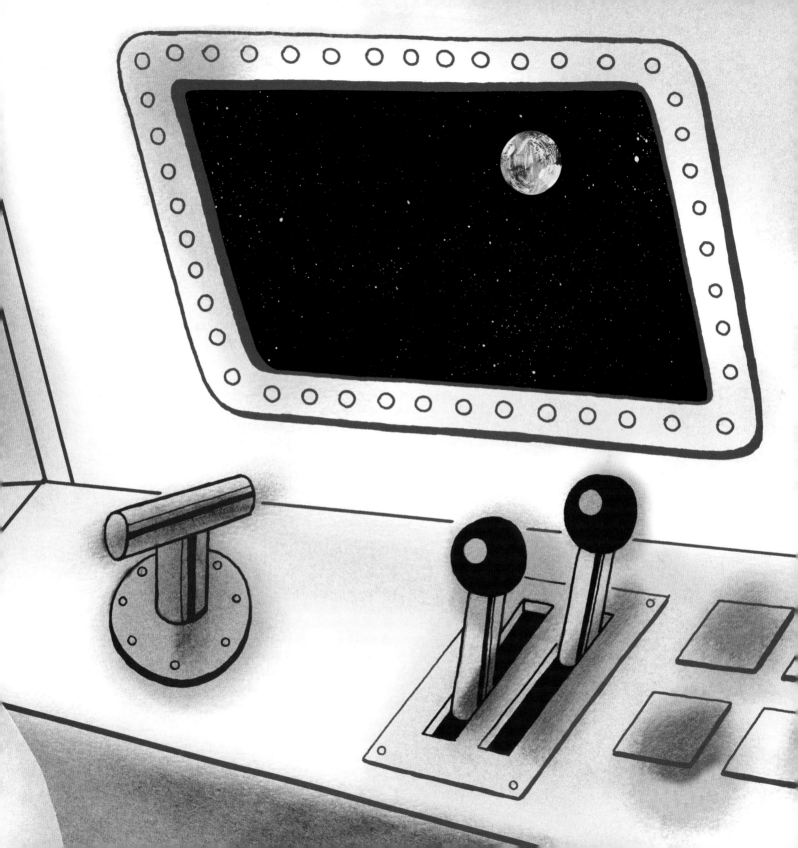

Fasten helmets,
gloves, and boots.
Backpacks, air tanks,
bulky suits.

Spacecraft readied.
System checks.
Lunar module

disconnects.

Michael Collins stays with ship. Waits, observing, tracking trip.

Nation watching,
bated breath.
Eagle landing—
life or death.

Armstrong makes his
one small step.
Giant leap from
years of prep.

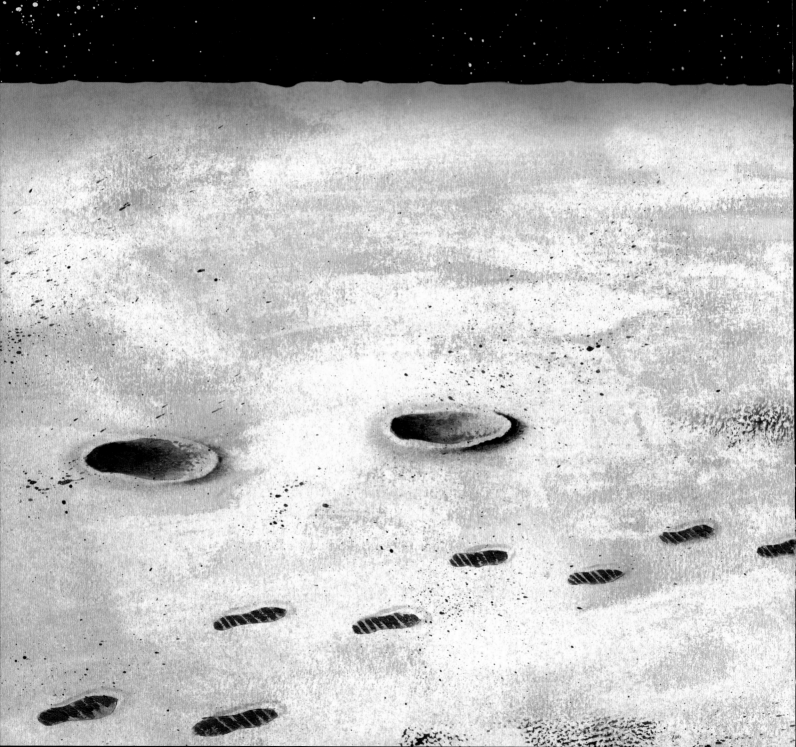

Edwin Aldrin
hops around.
Boot prints left on
ashen ground.

Desolation.
Silent. Dark.
Tranquil sea.
Barren. Stark.

Haul equipment.
Careful test.
Exploration.
Lunar quest.

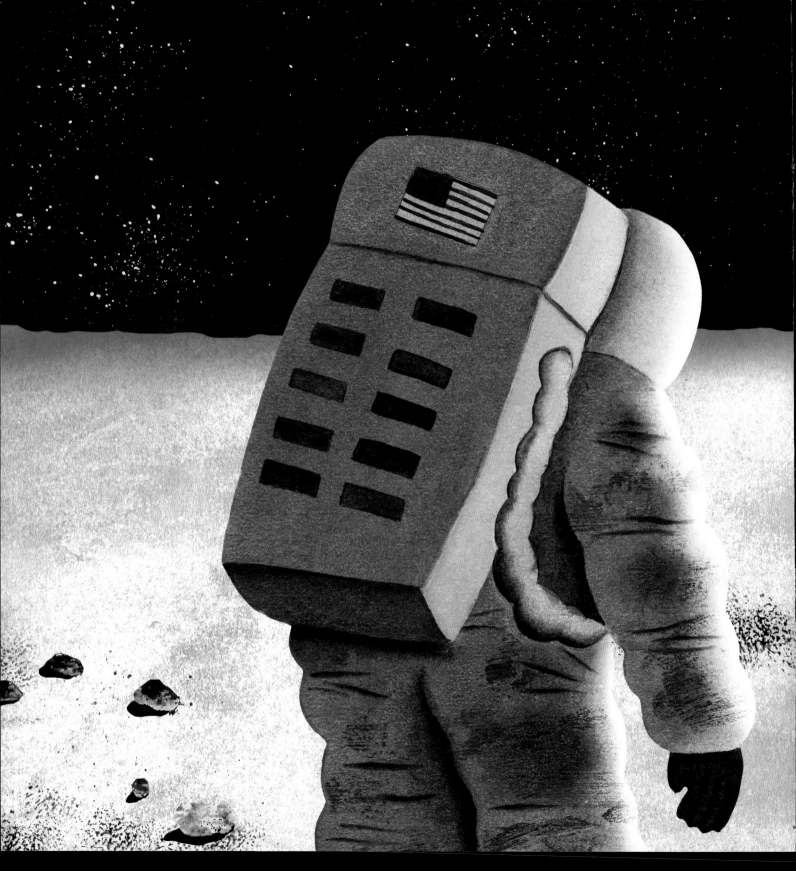

Snapping pictures,
planting flag.
Soil samples,
rocks in bag.

Eagle docking—
mission ends.
Journey home to
family, friends.

Swiftly speeding.
Earth ahead.
Ship arriving.
News is spread.

Ocean splashdown.
Heroes seen.
Helicopter.
Quarantine.

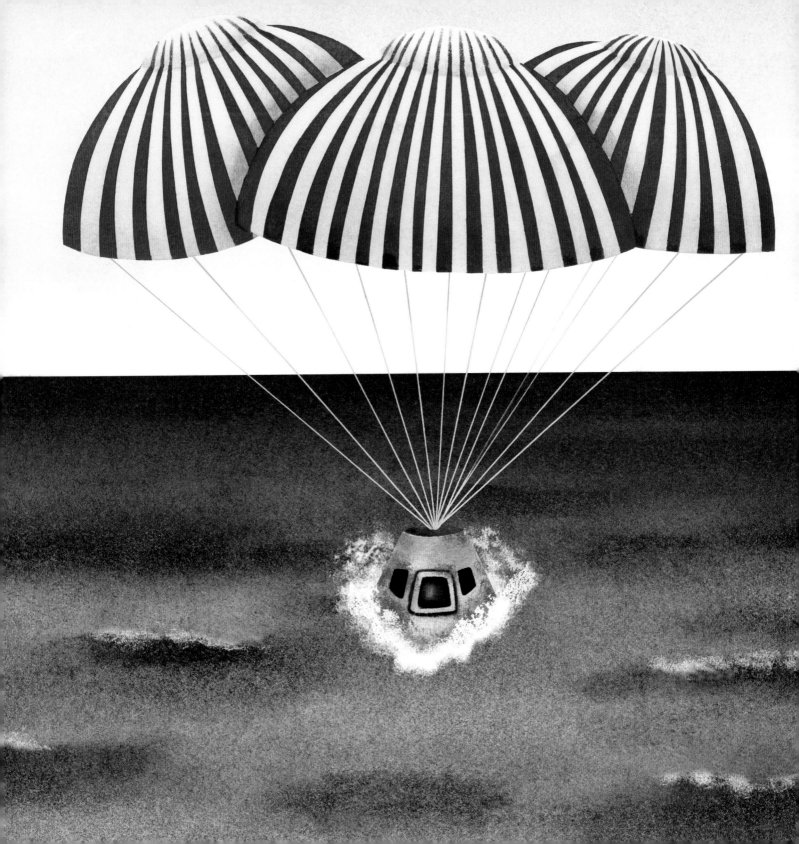

Brave explorers—
safe return.
Data gathered.
Much to learn.

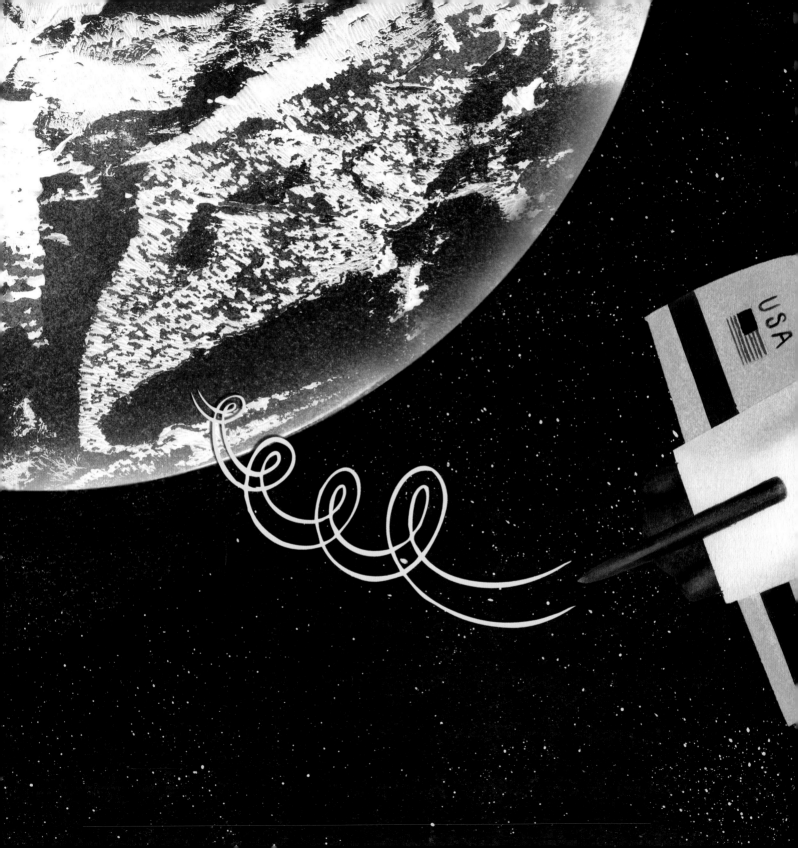

Lunar mission
reached new heights.
Paved the way
for future flights.

Author's Note

On July 16, 1969, the Apollo 11 mission to the moon began with the launch of a Saturn V rocket from Kennedy Space Center in Florida. After being thrust through space, the command module, *Columbia*, and the lunar module, *Eagle*, separated from the rocket and headed for the moon. On board were three astronauts: Neil Armstrong, Edwin "Buzz" Aldrin, and Michael Collins.

On July 20, *Eagle* detached from *Columbia* and made its descent to the lunar surface. Collins remained aboard *Columbia*, orbiting the moon, while the other two astronauts landed *Eagle* on an area of the moon called the Sea of Tranquility.

Armstrong and Aldrin performed scientific tests and collected samples of soil and rock. After two and a half hours, the astronauts planted an American flag as a reminder of their visit and left the lunar surface.

Eagle rejoined *Columbia*, and the crew began its journey home. Once *Columbia* reentered the Earth's atmosphere, parachutes opened and safely lowered the module into the Pacific Ocean. The crew was picked up by helicopter and taken to the *USS Hornet*, a nearby recovery ship.

Because traveling to the moon had never been done before, scientists were uncertain whether it would have any negative effects on humans. The astronauts were put in quarantine until it was determined that they were not sick from their journey. While in quarantine, the heroes were visited by President Richard M. Nixon.

Although the entire mission lasted only eight days, its historic nature makes it one of the most famous missions of the space program. It also fulfilled President John F. Kennedy's dream of sending a man to the moon and bringing him safely back to Earth before the end of the 1960s.

This photo shows the lunar module ascent prior to its docking with the command module. Photo date: July 21, 1969. Photo source: NASA.